Also by X. J. Kennedy

One Winter Night in August
and Other Nonsense Jingles
(*A Margaret K. McElderry Book*)

THE PHANTOM
ICE CREAM MAN

X. J. KENNEDY

THE PHANTOM
ICE CREAM MAN

More Nonsense Verse

Illustrated by David McPhail

A MARGARET K. MC ELDERRY BOOK

ATHENEUM   1979   NEW YORK

Library of Congress Cataloging
in Publication Data

Kennedy, X. J.
The phantom ice cream man.
"A Margaret K. McElderry book."
SUMMARY: A collection of nonsense verses about
Unheard-Of Birds, Couldn't-Be Beasts, Magical
Menaces, a Far-Out Family, and other topics.
1. Nonsense-verses, American. [1. Nonsense
verses] I. McPhail, David M. II. Title.
PZ8.3.K384Ph 811'.5'4 78-23681
ISBN 0-689-50132-3

Published simultaneously in Canada by McClelland & Stewart, Ltd.
Manufactured by
American Book–Stratford Press, Inc.,
Saddle Brook, New Jersey

First Edition

*For all who cherish Center School
of Bedford, Massachusetts*

ACKNOWLEDGMENTS

Some of these verses first appeared in *Cricket, Harper's, The New York Kid's Catalog* (Doubleday), Daisy Wallace's *Giant Poems* and *Ghost Poems* (Holiday House), and *The Inkspot* (Franklin Elementary School, Lexington, Massachusetts).

CONTENTS

Unheard-Of Birds and Couldn't-Be Beasts

A CHOOSY WOLF

"Why won't you eat me, wolf?" I asked.

"It wouldn't be much fun to.
Besides, I'm into natural foods
That nothing has been done to."

THE GARGOYLE'S PROTEST

Out of the gargoyle's throat of stone
    The overflowing waters
Keep gurgling in a monotone.
    It holds its head and mutters,

"I'm tired of looking down on boats!
    I'm going to complain
That even gargoyles get sore throats
    From gargling winter rain."

THE NINETEENTH-MOON-OF-NEPTUNE BEASTS

Who lives on Neptune's nineteenth moon?
How are its ski conditions?
Oh, why have we never heard one word
From the previous expeditions?

We skim low for a look around
And splash down. While untwisting
Our airlock door I catch the sound
Of infant beasts insisting,

"Please, Mom, can't we have something else?
Yes honestly, we've *tried*,
But these screwy eggs with rockets on
Have funny bugs inside!"

A CERTAIN SANDPIPER

I knew a tiny sandpiper
(Indeed, I know him yet)
Who wrapped his toes in sandpaper
So he wouldn't get them wet.

Now shod in scratchy shoes he goes
To soothe a whale who's stranded,
And he is why the shiny shore
Is always smoothly sanded.

THE LOCOMOTIVE SLOTH

Along train tracks, with yawning jaws,
He lies, this evil lummock,
Till locomotives pulling cars
Steam straight into his stomach.

Conductors, taken by surprise
At whizzing through the thickets
Of the Sloth's tonsils, tongue, and teeth,
Forget to take up tickets.

Cabooses make the best desserts.
His tight belt he unhitches,
And having eaten till he hurts,
He picks his teeth with switches.

The Sloth waxed sleek in days gone by
When locomotives flourished,
But now that they're in short supply,
He's growing undernourished.

A CONFUSED CHAMELEON

"Balls of fire!" cried chameleon Betty,
 "I'm so mixed up I'm ready to bust!
I got hit with a bunch of confetti—
 Now my color control won't adjust!"

THE DISCONTENTED COW

Mooed Maude, "I'm in the mood for food!
Bananas, please—on branflakes!
This old green grass just gives me gas—
Me for some pizza pancakes!

"Bring candied yams!
      Bring steamer clams!
Bring on the bratwurst, kid!—
Though this may mean my milk-machine
Will think I've flipped my lid."

THE X BIRD

The X bird is no bird at all.
It cannot lay an egg,
And as for stuff for standing on,
It hasn't got a leg.

No feathers flutter on its back,
It's never on the wing.
In fact, you'd think (if you weren't sure)
There could be no such thing.

THE MUDDLEHEADED MESSER

The wackiest bird
That you ever have heard
    Is the Muddleheaded Messer!
It warbles and squawks
As it rumples the socks
    In the drawer of a person's dresser.

If you ever should search
For a shirt for church
    And your drawer looks as though some bear
Went and muddled your clothes,
You can surely suppose
    That a Messer has nested there.

TYRANNOSAURUS REX'S TEETH

Tyrannosaurus Rex's teeth
Were pearly-white and porous.
To file their points
He'd chomp on joints
Of pachycephalosaurus.

"Why, Ty, your teeth are total wrecks!
They'll need a ton of drilling!"—
So Ty yawned wide
And Doc McBride
Supplied him with a filling.

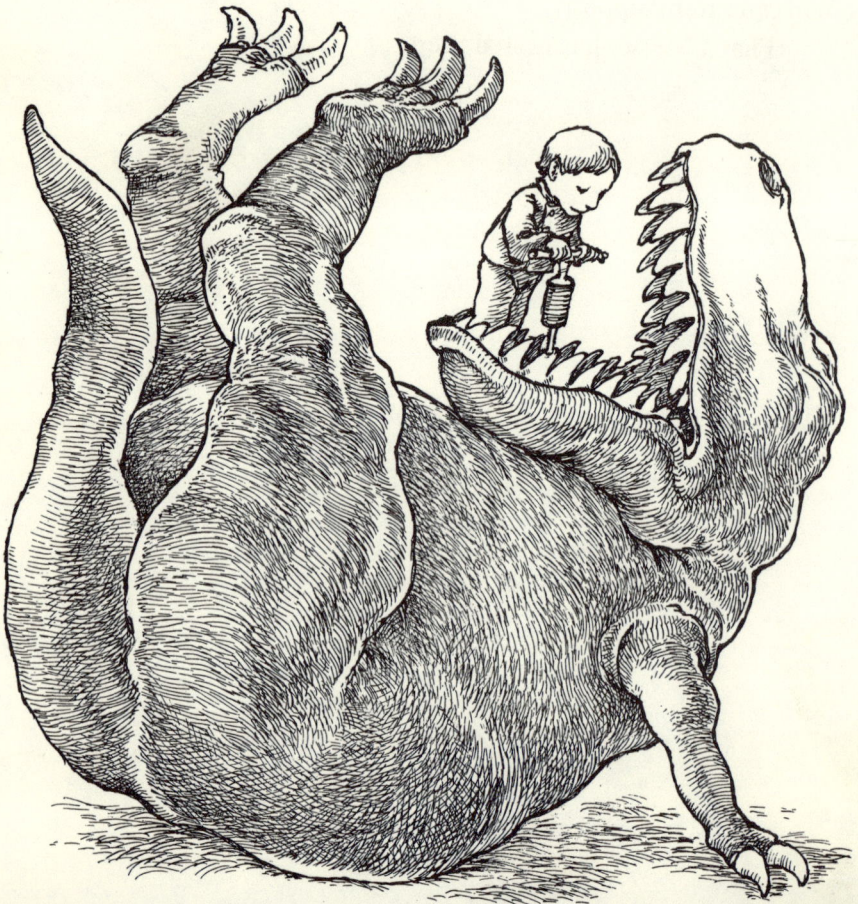

MACKEREL MACK AND HALIBUT HAL

Mackerel Mack and Halibut Hal
Were the two best buddies in the fish corral.
They rode bucking dolphins, herded rods and reels,
And they rounded up stray lightbulbs for electric eels.

But hard times fell on the old fish spread
(Lots of landlubbers liked grape jelly instead),
So one day, while they perched on a sunken barge,
Wondered Hal, "Shall we go see the sea at large?"

"Now you're talking!" cried Mack with a whale of a grin,
"Let's shake on it, partner!"—he stuck out a fin.
Then they saddled and mounted two tuna fish nags
And they packed two sponges for their saddlebags.

At the old Sand Bar next to Octopus Reef
They dismounted at dusk for some barbecued beef—
No, no—barbecued *squid*. And whom should they meet
But a tin-fin gambler named Pickerel Pete.

Now, Pete was an hombre who liked grand slams:
He thought nothing of betting a hundred clams,
And he leered, "Howdy, strangers—game o' high card stud?"
Answered Mack, "We're feeding." Said Hal, "Beat it, bud."

Well, Pickerel Pete flashed a needle-toothed jaw:
"No poor fish says *that* to me, strangers! Draw!"
And he fired a harpoon with intent to kill,
But it bounced off a bubble on the halibut's gill.

Muttered Mackerel Mack, "Durn your wigglin' tail,
You have come to the end of a one-way trail!"
While Halibut Hal (for still water runs deep)
Said nothing—just grinned as he made a leap.

In a wild waterwheel all three tails spun round
Lashing salt into foam! At that terrible sound
All the little shrimps ran to look on with dread.
Even ancient oysters got out of bed.

Mack and Hal fought hard, and the outcome was sweet:
Soon all that remained of Pickerel Pete
When at last they could see through a dust-eclipse
Was a kettle of chowder and some fish and chips.

Then those two tired pals, on their scaly steeds,
Off over a prairie of tumbling weeds,
Rode into the sunset and never came back.
Halibut Hal and Mackerel Mack.

Nonsensical Notions

LASAGNA

Wouldn't you love
To have lasagna
Any old time
The mood was on ya?

DINOSAUR DIN

Did stegosaurus bellow
Like a longhorn steer from Texas?
Could a bird's sweet tweet
Conceivably beat
Tyrannosaurus rex's?

Did pterodactyl cackle?
Did brachiosaurus bray?
Did monoclonius toot
Through his horny snoot
Ta ra ra boom de ay?

Did little lambeosauruses baa
Or bay like hounds in chorus?
Did the ankles clank
Like an army tank
Upon ankylosaurus?

Today, cars, planes and subway trains
Make a hubbubish hullabaloo
But the rumble and roar
Of a dinosaur
I never have heard. Have you?

I BRUSH MY TEETH WITH OCEAN SAND

I brush my teeth with ocean sand
    Against my dentist's wishes.
        In fact it drives him up the wall
        When in my mouth tides rise and fall
And every time I smile there stand
    Sand castles full of fishes
    And a little clam
            (who squishes).

JANE GAVE A LEAP FROM HER TRAPEZE

Jane gave a leap from her trapeze
And Jack swung down to catch her,
But as she reached to take his hand
She felt a need to scratch her—

A need to scratch her—now, let's see,
Let's get our story right.
She had to scratch her where she itched
From a mosquito bite.

SWEPT OFF HIS PINS

Mister Malachi O'Malley
Rumbled down the bowling alley
In hardly any time at all,
His thumb stuck in his bowling ball,
And landed sweetly as you like—
Crash! bang! bongo!—perfect strike.

A LOT OF LIMERICKS

1 / *Sticky Situation*
    Muttered centipede Slither McGrew,
    "What on earth can I possibly do?
        Here I'm late for a date
        And foot seventy-eight
    Has some chewing gum stuck to its shoe!"

2 / *Odd Bird*
    The checkerboard-breasted toot-tooter
    Has a beak with a built-in beanshooter.
        While it feathers its nest
        Owls play chess on its chest
    And its chick brings canned string beans by scooter.

3 / A *Bright Idea*
    A pretentious old man of the Bosporus
    Used to cover his goat cart with phosphorus
        So that, driving by night
        He would get the green light
    And his goats would consider him prosperous.

4 / *Custer's Last Stand*

"I don't like this," said General Custer,
"How come every last man has missed muster?
 Was that somebody scary
 Peering over the prairie
And not just an old feather duster?"

5 / *In-flight Meal*

A wicked rich witch named Fat Wadda
Wished to dine on her way to Nevada,
 But a broomstick in flight
 Isn't much fun to bite,
So she sat on a hot enchilada.

6 / *Television Charmer*

Said a mouthful of Mighty Mump cereal,
"All I am is mere lumps of material—
 Sugar, corncobs, and dye,
 But when televised I
Am made up to look simply ethereal!"

7 / *A Visit to the Gingerbread House*

"Why, sit down!" (So I let myself settle
In a fudge chair.) "I'll put on the kettle,"
 Purred the witch. "Here, just try
 Some delicious toad pie
And a cup of hot Hansel and Gretel!"

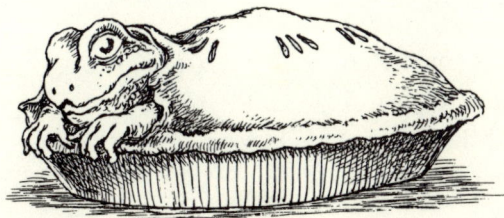

SHOULD ALL OF THIS COME TRUE

If combs could brush their teeth,
If a needle's eye shed tears,
If bottles craned their necks,
If corn pricked up its ears,

If triangles held their sides
And laughed, if down the street
A mile like a millipede
Ran by on wavy feet,

If cans of laundry lye
Declared they tell no fibs,
If baked potatoes dug
Umbrellas in the ribs,

If sheets of rain were starched,
If a brook, with mutterings,
Rolled over in its bed
With a deep creek of springs,

Should all of this come true
And all time were to pass,
Then you could slice a piece of cheese
With any blade of grass.

Magical
Menaces

WICKED WITCH ADMIRES HERSELF

"Mirror, mirror on the wall,
Whose is the fairest face of all?
I'll come close, so you'll see me clearer—"

Pop! goes another magic mirror.

THE UP-TO-DATE GIANT

I'm all caught up, I'm where things are!
    I've swapped my old self-strumming
Harp for an amplified guitar.
    No more fee-fi-fo-fumming.

I can't stand Englishmen's ground bones,
    They clog my cookie cutter,
And golden eggs taste—yuk!—like stones.
    Please pass the peanut butter.

HICKENTHRIFT AND HICKENLOOP

Hickenthrift and Hickenloop
    Stood fourteen mountains high.
They'd wade the wind, they'd have to stoop
    To let the full moon by.

Their favorite sport, played on a court,
    Was called Kick Down the Castle—
They'd stamp their boots, those vast galoots,
    Till king lay low as vassal.

One day while spooning hot rock soup
    From a volcano crater,
Said Hickenthrift, "Say, Hickenloop,
    Who of us two is greater?"

Across the other's jagged brow
    Dark thunder seemed to drift
And Hickenloop, with one swift swoop,
    Ate straight through Hickenthrift.

THE ABOMINABLE BASEBALL BAT

I swung and swung at empty air
And when I heard the umpire
Behind me shout, "Strike three—you're out!"
My bat turned to a vampire.

The whole team had to pry it loose.
Poor Ump looked sort of flat.
Now ever since, my bat and I
Walk every time we bat.

THE SASQUATCH QUASHES A RUMOR

My bigfoot friend Bill Bunyan
    Who's shy and hard to meet
Stands taller than a mountain—
    That's in his stocking feet.

When people spy his footprints
    They run. Says Bill, "What bosh!
The only thing a sasquatch
    Will eat is summer squash."

TERRIBLE TROLL'S TOLLBRIDGE

(Try saying this title ten times rapidly.)

"Aw, enough is enough!"
Said the Billygoats Gruff,
    And their neighbor the Terrible Troll
Said, "You're welcome to pass
To the hill to crop grass
    If you'll pay me a reasonable toll."

Now they screech to a stop
At his toll bridge and drop
    Goatsmilk cheeses between the troll's choppers.
Old Troll charges a cheese
For a little goat, please—
    Two for mediums, three for big whoppers.

TWO DOORBELLS

Two doorbells glowered out at me
With buttons big and bright.
Which one to push? Was it the left
Or the right one that was right?

I plucked up courage, pushed the right,
I pushed it good and strong—
An angry eagle came. Good night!
I must have rung dead wrong!

He shrieked, "I've flown down one whole flight
Of stairs, you runt! Pray tell,
What makes you think you've got a right
To wrong me and my bell?"

He slammed the door so hard it left
My glasses with no glass.
Well, I gave the left-hand bell a press—
Right soon, a braying ass,

A rhino with his rump on wrong,
A tribe of owls that sang
An odd, foul-sounding sort of song,
A red orang-utang,

A mummy coming all unwrapped
And a huge blue shark replied.
The shark, his jawbones open, snapped:
"Why don't you step inside?"

I turned toes right around and left,
Which didn't take me long.
I'd got the number right, all right,
But that street was downright wrong.

MY DRAGON

I have a purple dragon
With a long brass tail that clangs,
And anyone not nice to me
Soon feels his fiery fangs,

So if you tell me I'm a dope
Or call my muscles jelly,
You just might dwell a billion years
Inside his boiling belly.

My
Far-Out
Family

A TICKLISH RECIPE

"These sourpusses," says Aunt Jill,
"Can use a few good tickles!"—

So that's why she puts stalks of dill
In jars of homemade pickles.

ALARM

Mother come quick!
Robert looks sick!
He opened the shoe polish, took a big lick!

It's worse than I feared!
He's grown a brown beard!
All four walls, the floor, and the ceiling are smeared!

Come look and see!
Don't you wish he
Was never a trouble to people, like me?

A BIG DEAL FOR THE TOOTH FAIRY

Tooth Fairy, hear! Tonight's the night
    I've dreamed about for ages,
For haven't we kids got a right
    To rake in living wages?

I've tried to work my back teeth loose,
    Tied doorknobs (threads—what cop-outs!),
But gosh! my jaws just won't produce
    A quick cash crop of dropouts.

So come prepared to lose a heap
    In larger trading ventures.
Tonight I lay me down to sleep
    On top of Grandpop's dentures.

MY MOTHER'S MAD FOR BARGAIN SALES

My mother's mad for bargain sales—
      At any slice in prices
Her eyeballs whiz like roulette wheels.
      One night we had a crisis

When Father, studying the bills,
      Exclaimed, "Great gravy, Myrtle!
You bought six paper swimming pools
      For a petrified sea turtle?"

But Mother just looked innocent
      And rolled her gaze toward heaven:
"Why, George, you skinflint! all I spent
      Was a dollar ninety-seven!"

She'd bought backscratchers for a pig
      ("Aunt Susan's Soothing Itch-Porks"),
Iron rubbers guaranteed to rust
      For when it's raining pitchforks,

An air-cooled sunspot-staining kit,
      Some school clothes for my kitty,
A map of Minneapolis
      Far larger than its city,

And last, for her own lower limbs,
      A sharkskin bathing skirt.
Now everywhere that Mother swims
      She's nicknamed Mermaid Myrt.

MY DELICATESSEN-LOVING DOG

My dog's a deli-loving dog:
He's crazy like a fox.
He sneers if I put bread
Upon his nose and tell him *Roll!*—
He says, "You call that thing a roll?
And also, where's the lox?"

He'll only speak for liver paste,
He'll sit up straight to beg
For salami,
Hot pastrami,
And a purple pickled egg.

IN THE MOTEL

Bouncing! bouncing! on the beds
My brother Bob and I cracked heads—

People next door heard the crack,
Whammed on the wall, so we whammed right back.

Dad's razor caused an overload
And wow! did the TV set explode!

Someone's car backed fast and—tinkle!
In our windshield was a wrinkle.

Eight more days on the road? Hooray!
What a bang-up holiday!

MAKING WORK FOR FATHER

To hit a bump is what I like
So Father has to fix my bike.

Both handlebars a total wreck,
I wear the pedals round my neck.

Then Father, in an awful tizzy,
Swings the hound round till they both drop dizzy,

Scowls at my owl,
Growls at my mink,
Bites a big hole through the kitchen sink,
Kicks kindling wood from his workbenches,

And goes and gets his monkey wrenches.

THE CAT WHO ASPIRED TO HIGHER THINGS

Our cat turns up her nose at mice.
She thinks rhinoceroses
Are twice as nice as mice to chase,
But now the mice are everyplace,

In the furnace,
In the freezer,
In Aunt Edith's orange squeezer,

In the cellar,
In the cider,
In Great-Grandpa's best hang-glider,

In the ginger,
In the allspice,
In Aunt Flora's King Kong false face,

In the stamps,
In the chocolate section
Of my ice cream cone collection—

All four of my uncle Erics
Tear their hair and throw hysterics.
Father smashes chairs and cusses.

At least we've no rhinoceroses.

MOTHER'S PIG

My mother has a spotted pig.
She treats it mean and rotten.
She pokes its skin all full of pins.
(It's gingham stuffed with cotton.)

One day while reconstructing shirts
My mother sure was shaken
To hear that pig yell, "Yow, that hurts,
You big pain in the bacon!"

COUSIN CARREES CUBIC CUISINE

Carrée my cousin's
Long on tricks:
She shapes ground round
To perfect bricks,

Six-sided roast-
Beef hash she slings.
Right-angled come
Her onion rings!

Because she carves
While she computes,
Her carrot sticks
Are real square roots.

She'll slice nice cubes
Of cool cucumber
And dice you fries
That roll a number,

Squeeze burger buns
To squares and squeal:
"Ding-ding! come get
Your good square meal!"

THE PRIZE IN THE SKY

When my uncle Bob Boone
Won a flying balloon
    Guessing how many beans in a jar,
He cried, "Hip hip hooray!"
And skipped home all the way
    From the annual 4-H bazaar.

When his pet billy goat
Bites a rope, off we float
    To a sky full of cottony clouds
And for ballast Unk packs
Buttered popcorn in sacks
    That we drop to uproarious crowds.

Here we go overseas!
Over tender green trees!
    Oh, what wonderful eyefuls of seeing!
Then, suspended from ropes,
Down the steep tinted slopes
    Of a rainbow our basket goes wheeeeeeing!

Cheerful
Spirits

THE HAUNTED OVEN

You're not supposed to roast a ghost
Or baste its half-baked bedsheet,
But every time my Mom makes bread—
EEEK!—stuck fast to the breadsheet

Is something bad that will not rise
(Poor Pop throws fits of jitters),
Just loafing there with rolly eyes,
Emitting crumby titters.

DIPLODOCUS HOLIDAY

One night in a dark museum
While a dusty old clock struck *one*
Two diplodocus skeletons
Who wanted to have some fun

Stepped stiffly from their pedestals
On toenails gray and hazy
And grabbed some stegosaurus skulls
And bowled down bones like crazy!

They rock-and-rolled around the room
Making showcases rattle,
They rode a dodo piggyback—
A fossil cried, "I'll tattle!"

But those diplodocus ghosts replied
In voices thin as paper,
"It's too darn long now since we died—
High time we cut a caper!"

One seized a pterodactyl's tail
That didn't have much feeling
And glided it until it bashed
A big hole through the ceiling.

They munched some million-year-old eggs
That made their belches dusty.
"What crust!" one groaned. "At making meals
I feel a trifle rusty."

Then, hearing Will the watchman's steps,
They gave two leaps and froze
Back upon their home pedestals
In innocent repose.

Old Will's suspicious flashlight shone
And long he stood there thinking.
Those two stuffed chuckles down their throats
(Though they couldn't keep from winking).

"I could have sworn—" said baffled Will,
But all looked quite all right
In that musty old museum room
In the middle of dark night.

WHOSE BOO IS WHOSE?

Two ghosts I know once traded heads
And shrieked and shook their sheets to shreds—
"You're me!" yelled one, "and me, I'm you!
Now who can boo the loudest boo?"

"Me!" cried the other, and for proof
He booed a boo that scared the roof
Right off our house. Our TV set
Jumped higher than a jumbo jet.

The first ghost snickered. "Why, you creep,
Call that a boo? that feeble beep?
Hear *this!*"—and sucking in a blast
Of wind, he puffed his sheet so vast

And booed so hard, a passing goose
Lost all its down. The moon shook loose
And fell and smashed to smithereens—
Stars scattered like spilled jellybeans.

"How's that for booing, boy? I win,"
Said one. The other scratched a chin
Where only bone was—"Win or lose?
How can we tell whose boo is whose?"

ATTIC GHOSTS

An awful laugh
Like crackling static
Keeps drifting
From our dark old attic

And when it rains
You'll hear the clinking
Of ten-ton chains.
It starts me thinking

That all our bad
Badminton rackets
I whacked rocks with,
All those seed packets

I didn't sell,
Those half-made gliders
Might just as well
Collect more spiders.

THE PHANTOM ICE CREAM MAN

When frost unlocks the last stiff leaf
And autumn stars start twinkling,
The North Wind's wolf pack prowls our street.
On such nights I've an inkling

Of someone strange. I catch my breath
Between chill bedsheets, hearing
The far-off tingle of his bell
Now faint, but slowly nearing . . .

Then why not raise the window shade
And look? Oh no, I daren't
For fear I'll see a man in white
On a truck dim and transparent.

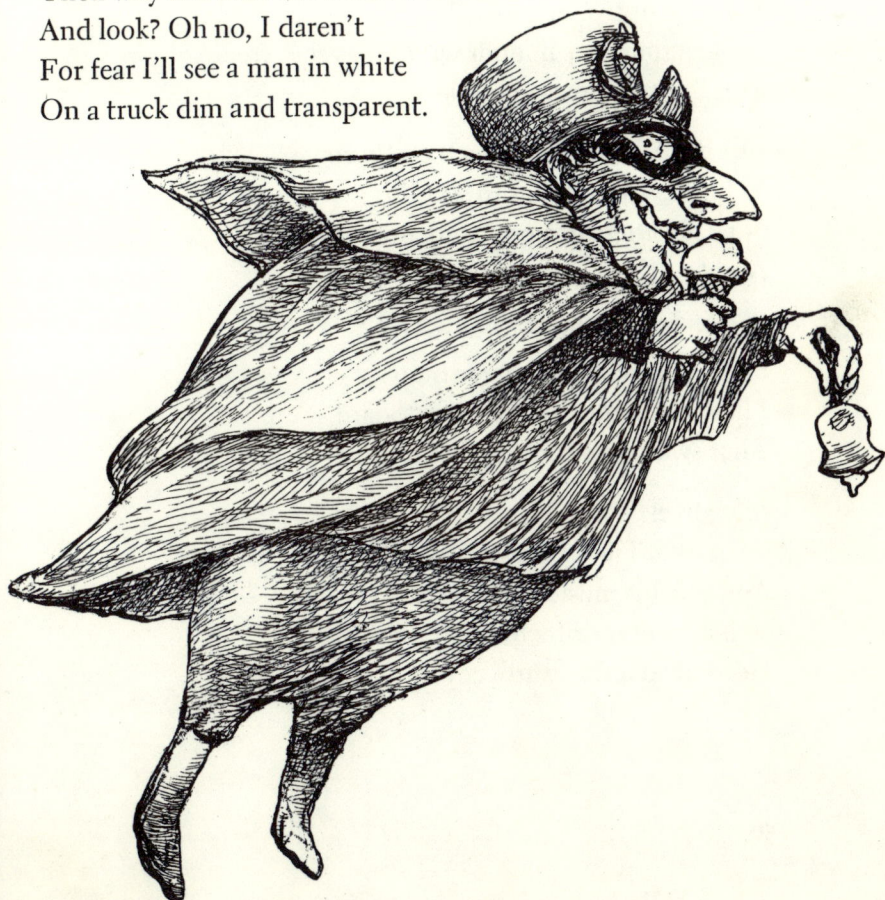

He calls in sweetly wheedling tones,
Familiar, almost human,
"Frostsicles? Frozen yogurt cones?
Who'll try my chocolate snowmen?"

Taste ice cream from another world
And you'll become a phantom,
Be seized by hands of breeze, be swirled
With dizzying momentum

To lands of everlasting ice
Where, captive in his castle,
Ringed round by hounds with fangs that freeze,
You'll try to move a muscle

But can't. Who'd buy such costly cones?
Yet his cry sets things to seeming:
Now old enchantments walk my room
And breathe. Can I be dreaming?

I smell mown clover's lost perfume,
Hear pigeons flute and murmur.
I hear once more the creaking board
That swung me through last summer—

July alive!
                    Then far away
And soft his music hovers.
White winter drifts to earth. I draw
Head deep inside warm covers.